300

Great Grand Prix Facts

For Motorsport Fans

All Facts are correct as of
April 2th 2022

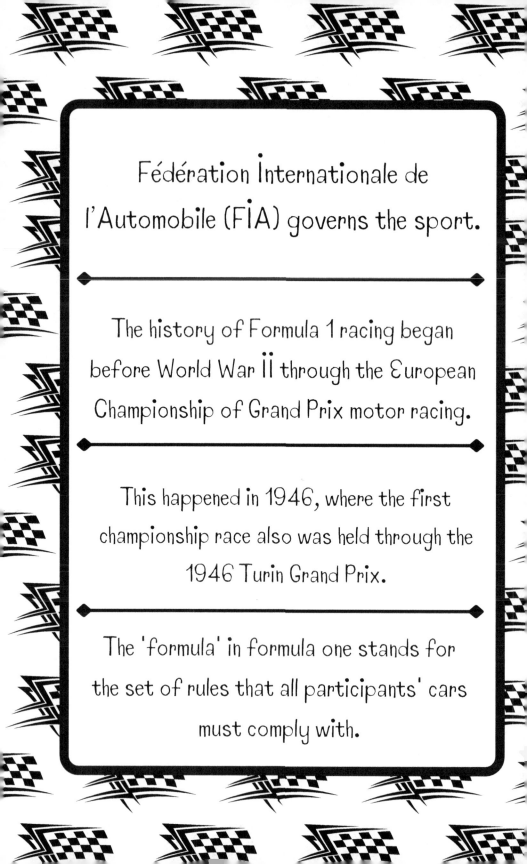

Fédération Internationale de l'Automobile (FIA) governs the sport.

The history of Formula 1 racing began before World War II through the European Championship of Grand Prix motor racing.

This happened in 1946, where the first championship race also was held through the 1946 Turin Grand Prix.

The 'formula' in formula one stands for the set of rules that all participants' cars must comply with.

The number "1" in the name entails the highest classification in the formula racing tournaments.

There are Formula Two, Formula Three, Formula Four, and Formula Students for lower classes in the sport.

An average F1 car can accelerate from 0 to 100MPH and go back to zero in just four seconds.

An F1 car is an "open wheel, open-cockpit, single-seat racing car."

Stefano Domenicali is an Italian manager and the current CEO of Formula One Group, replacing Chase Carey.

A Formula 1 clutch is different any other clutches. It is less than half the size of ordinary clutches, is a special carbon-carbon design and can be subject (at times) to almost 1,000 degrees of heat.

The onboard cameras on F1 cars are coloured differently to distinguish between 2 members of the same team.

An F1 car is an "open wheel, open-cockpit, single-seat racing car."

The first car in a team will have a black camera and the second a fluorescent yellow one.

In the pit lane it is not permissible to use powered devices to lift the cars. All jacks for example must be manual.

Small planes are able to take off at slower speeds than F1 cars reach during a race.

An average household car revs up to 6,000 rpm (revolutions per minute), an F1 engine usually revs up to 18,000 rpm.

The front suspension of an F1 car can cope with up to 2 tonnes of pressure.

Once a race has finished an F1 car's tyres will still be hot enough to cook an egg on (around 120° centigrade).

A Formula 1 engine is so finely tuned that it can't be turned over when it is cold.

Warm oil and water are pumped through the cars first to allow the metals to expand.

Since 1999 it has been compulsory for wheels on Formula 1 cars to be tethered to the car

---

The tiny struts turn the car, and also provide suspension. They're adjustable to reflect the demands of different circuits.

The diffuser is a flared area at the rear of the car that creates downforce, keeping the car on the road or track.

Safety is crucial in F1, and a tubular titanium structure called a halo protects drivers from large objects and debris during races.

F1 brakes heat up to more than 1,000 degrees Celsius, and they require huge force and finesse from drivers to work effectively.

Drivers sit horizontally in their cockpits in seats moulded to their bodies, with pedals towards the front of the car.

Pirelli's 2022 tyres are 18 inches in size — far larger than the 13-inch wheels used on older cars.

The sidepods house radiators to cool the power unit. They're aerodynamic, and they're made from deformable material to improve safety.

An F1 car's rear wing is crucial for aerodynamic stability.

F1 cars use hybrid power units with 1.6-litre engines that run at 15,000rpm; each driver has three per season.

Each race in a season is called a 'Grand Prix' or GP and all the races in a season combined are called 'Grands Prix'.

The minimum total distance of a Grand Prix race, including all the pre-defined number of laps must be 300 km or 190 miles.

There is a standard distance for all races except for the Monaco GP which is 260 km or 160 miles.

The sport has a massive following across the world that records 500 million viewers annually.

F1 cars have been known to reach peak speeds of 300 kmph or 185 mph on an average.

Pit lane speed limits vary during events (usually 100km/h) but are set at 60km/h for all free practice sessions.

When a driver pulls into a pit stop, that means it is time for high speed tire changing.

"Red Bull Racing" holds the record for the fastest time having registered a time of 2.05 seconds at the start of the 2013 season.

An F1 team can have around 600 people working hard to make sure everything goes right and according to plan.

Racers' suits are designed to protect them from flames and burns and are made to the specifications of NASA.

The material used for drivers suits is Nomex Fibre which "can survive temperature of around 700-800 degrees Celsius for more than 10 seconds".

The first race of 2022 takes place in Bahrain on March 20 and this season will be the longest ever, with 23 races.

Formula 1 races take place on Sundays and usually last about two hours.

Qualifying, which takes place on Saturdays, determines the starting order for the Sunday race.

Teams use different tyres during races: softer tyres provide more grip but deteriorate quickly, while harder tyres have less grip but last longer.

No tyres last for a full race, though, so teams must decide when to stop their cars to fit a new set.

The driver with the fastest lap during the race gets an extra point.

The top ten drivers in each F1 race receive points

F1 racers lose over 3 litres of body water during 1 race.

Car tires lose 0.5kgs during a race.

The F1 Helmets are the toughest in the world.

The average F1 racer loses 4 kg during a race.

Weight of an F1 car must be over 728kg (without fuel).

The lifespan of an F1 engine is less than 5 races.

The average F1 pit stop is currently around 2.5 seconds.

F1 cars rev at 15,000 RPM.

The fastest speed ever achieved by an F1 car is 397.360km/h, set by the Honda F1 team back in 2006, in a modified version of their 2005 car on the Bonneville Salt Flats in the USA.

Juan Fangio is the oldest winner of the World Drivers' Championship; he was 46 years and 41 days old when he won the 1957 title.

Engineers assemble 80,000 components for just one car.

Due to the intense heat from the F1 car and the cockpit, the drivers must stay hydrated during the race.

There is a water pouch attached to a driver's helmet, and with just one press on a button, they can drink the available water.

On average, F1 cars with a driver weigh at least 740kgs.

Experts claim that F1 cars can be driven upside down given that it has the best components, but the primary source of this is the aerodynamic force of F1 cars.

F1 engines require several complex conditions that road cars can't process or handle.

Michael Schumacher and Lewis Hamilton now hold the record with the most wins in the entire Formula 1 World Drivers' Championship history at 7 championships.

It was only in 1958 when the first woman held the steering wheel of an F1 car during a race — Maria Teresa de Felippis.

In the Grand Prix's entire history, only one woman has scored a point, and that is the Italian driver, Lella Lombardi.

Max Verstappen was only 17 years old (youngest driver) when he first competed in a Formula 1 racing competition.

With 20 championship wins in total, the United Kingdom proved its dominance in the sport.

Ferrari is the best engine manufacturer in F1 history based on its record of winning 15 championships.

At present, there are 52 fatalities recorded. FIA does its best to have tight regulations for drivers' safety.

Kevlar fuel tanks and fiberglass bulkheads have saved many F1 drivers over the years.

Fireproof suits are an essential piece of F1 safety gear.

Trailing medical cars are the world's fastest ambulances.

The crash helmet is the most important pieces of safety kit.

The helmet is built using 120 mats of high-performance carbon fibre T800, layer by layer, the tens of thousands of fibres of which are thinner than a human hair.

Helmets that are unable to resist a 3kg (6.6lbs) pointed metal object being dropped from a height of three-meters are rejected.

Chin straps must also not stretch more than 30mm (1.18-inch) when subjected to 38kg (84lbs) of stress.

There are more than 300 sensors on a Formula 1 car.

No two steering wheels are the same in Formula 1, with buttons, dials, paddles and even grip size honed to each driver's liking.

An F1 driver experiences double the g-force of an astronaut.

Just 3.340 kilometres long, the Monaco Grand Prix has the shortest track on the F1 calendar.

The Monaco Grand Prix circuit boasts the slowest corner in F1.

Brazilian born driver Ayrton Senna is the current record holder for number of Monaco Grand Prix wins. His total stands at 6 wins.

Each year, a whopping 33 kilometres of safety rails are set up.

3600 tyres are used for tyre barriers and 20,000 square metres of wire catch fencing.

The Monaco Grand Prix requires around six weeks to set up the track before the race and three weeks to remove it afterwards.

McLaren is the team who has won the most Monaco Grand Prix races.

The first Grand Prix at Silverstone since the 2020 season (and Covid-19 protocols) attracted a record-breaking 365,000.

Today Formula One, along with the Olympic games and the FIFA World Cup, is one of the most publicised events.

F1 driver numbers are allocated by ballot and drivers keep that number for the whole of their race career unless they are the champion.

All drivers who wish to compete in F1 must have a FIA Super Licence.

Every entering F1 driver with the surname of 'Hill' has won a championship (Graham, Damon and Phil).

After Ayrton Senna's fatal crash in 1994 staff found an Austrian flag in the Brazilian driver's car.

Because of the training required to deal with the g-forces involved in Formula 1 driving, F1 drivers tend to have disproportionately thick necks.

Formula 1 drivers are subject to random drugs tests.

Thirty three different drivers have won the Formula 1 Championship.

Queen Elizabeth II attended the very first Formula 1 race in 1950 with her father King George VI and sister Princess Margaret.

The last Formula 1 fatality during a race was Ayrton Senna who died after his crash at San Marino in 1994.

The driver's championship was discussed as early as 1930 but the advent of the Second World War put plans on hold until 1950.

In 1950 there were only 7 races in a season.

The country with the most F1 Championship winning drivers is the UK with 10 drivers.

Since the first Formula One Championship in 1950, 69 countries have hosted a Grand Prix.

For many years Juan Manuel Fangio held the record for the most World Championship titles (1951, 1954, 1955, 1956 and 1957).

In 1950 there were only 7 races in a season.

The country with the most F1 Championship winning drivers is the UK with 10 drivers.

Since the first Formula One Championship in 1950, 69 countries have hosted a Grand Prix.

For many years Juan Manuel Fangio held the record for the most World Championship titles (1951, 1954, 1955, 1956 and 1957).

Michael Schumacher broke the record of most championships won in 2003 when he won his 6th Championship.

The 1958 Formula 1 Championship experienced the most driver fatalities with four drivers losing their lives in track accidents.

In 1953, 34 cars lined up for the German Grand Prix making it the busiest Formula One race ever.

Manhole covers have to be welded down before the Monaco Grand Prix because the down force created by an F1 car has enough suction to pull them up.

The Italian circuit at Monza is particularly hard on F1 brakes. At the first corner drivers take just 2 seconds to decrease speed from 200 mph to 60 mph.

Woodcote at Silverstone was historically the first corner ever tackled in a Formula One race.

The Marina Bay Street Circuit in Singapore is raced at night and has nearly 1,500 lighting projectors to project the light from 2,000-watt white metal halide lamps.

The Yas Marina Circuit in Abu Dhabi has the longest acceleration period of any F1 track in the world at 1,173 metres.

Formula One teams bring special down force packages to the Monza track in Italy because it has such long straights and rapid deceleration.

The Bahrain International Circuit has numbers instead of the usual names for all of its corners except one.

The Turn 1 hairpin was renamed after Michael Schumacher because he was the first person to win the Bahrain Grand Prix.

Monaco is the shortest Formula One circuit at only 3,340 kilometres. This means that it has the highest number of laps at 78.

Whilst most of today's Formula One circuits are between 4 and 6 kilometres long, in 1957 the Pescara track in Italy was 25.579 kilometres.

The Nurburgring track in Germany was built to help provide employment for workers in the area. It took 25,000 people from 1925 to 1927 to construct.

F1 helmets can stand flames of 800° centigrade for at least 45 seconds.

In 1977 David Purley recorded the biggest impact during an F1 crash. His car at the British Grand Prix took only 2 seconds to go from 108 mph to standstill. The estimated resulting g-force was 197.8.

Every second a Formula 1 car driving in the wet displaces 250 litres of water.

F1 car chassis are made of extremely strong materials including Kevlar, metal, carbon fibre and structures similar to honeycomb.

Most F1 car tyres are filled with nitrogen because it has a more consistent air pressure than normal air.

The maximum pit lane speed allowed is 80 kph for most circuits. At Monaco it is 60 kph because the pit lane is so tight.

All F1 cars have a circuit breaker fitted inside the car so that in the event of a crash the driver can cut all of the main electrical circuits.

Should it be required, a safety car contains two people. An experienced circuit driver and an FIA observer who maintains contact with race control.

Mobile Formula 1 response teams include four salvage cars and two rescue cars. There are also two extraction teams.

All points on a track can be reached within 30 seconds.

The HANS (Head and Neck Support) device is a type of head restraint that was adopted by Formula 1 in 2003.

Netflix's Formula One documentary series vastly boosted viewership numbers in the US.

The 2021 season-opening Bahrain Grand Prix broke viewership records on Sky Sports.

Lewis Hamilton is the highest paid driver with an annal salary of $40 million.

Valued at $50.8 billion, Mercedes is the most valuable Formula 1 team brand.

Formula racing cars can get from 0 to 300 km/h in 10.6 seconds.

F1's cost cap has come down from $145million to $140m for the 2022 season, with another $5m reduction due next year.

Since 2010, Pirelli has been the sole supplier of Formula One tyres.

The Circuit de Spa-Francorchamps is the longest F1 racing track.

The Formula One Group recorded US$2.14 billion in revenue in 2021.

Formula 1 announced that it had struck a $100m deal to sell betting sponsorships.

Ongoing and blisteringly fast development means that a Formula 1 race car part is redesigned every 20 minutes.

over the duration of a race, about four of the race car's parts were redesigned back at the factory.

The front wing of an F1 wing is coated with Teflon so that rubber flying off other cars' tires doesn't stick to it and disturb airflow.

A front wing costs a staggering $275,000 to design and manufacture from carbon fibre.

A Tungsten steel material called Densamet is placed strategically for ballast.

More than 300 gigabits of data is downloaded from the car during a race weekend.

The steering wheel, with all its buttons and dials, has more than 500 possible settings.

The steering wheel in an F1 car typically costs around $85,000.

A mission control room at the Mercedes-AMG Petronas headquarters contains eight huge television screens and 90 computer monitors.

Drivers get a replica of the trophy won in a race; the race teams keep the originals. However, Hamilton's contract stipulates he gets to keep the originals.

In Formula 1, there are no regulations for the amount of power a team can use in their cars.

The specifications of an F1 engine are four-stroke, turbocharged 1.6-liter, 90-degree V6 turbo engines.

The maximum engine power rotational speed is 15,000 revolutions per minute (rpm).

Schumacher began racing with F1 with the Benetton F1 team in 1991.

Michael Schumacher has won 91 races from 308 entries.

Michael Schumacher won 8 out of 14 races in his first F1 championship win (1994).

Schumacher returned to racing in 2010 with Mercedes GP team, but he did not win any races before retiring in 2012.

Mercedes is considered to have the maximum Horse Power (HP). Ferrari comes next, with Renault and Honda have considerably gap over the two giants.

The total power of a F1 engine is measured after calculating the power in the V6 engines, and Energy Recovery System (ERS).

There are two types of Motor Generator Units — Kinetic (MGU-K) and Heat (MGU-H) in an F1 car.

The MGU-K collects and stores kinetic energy when the car is braking.

The MGU-H is connected to the turbocharger and harnesses waste energy from the exhaust, which contributes to the overall power.

The modern V6 turbo engines contain electric energy is stored in what is known as the Energy Store (ES).

The Indy 500 was also one of the inaugural races during the first 11 years of the modern Formula 1 World Championship (1950-60).

The Watkins Glen circuit near New York established a solid place on the F1 calendar for 20 consecutive years, from 1961-80.

A street circuit in Long Beach, California, hosted the United States Grand Prix West between 1975-83.

A 3.427-mile (5.515 km) circuit is situated on 890 acres (3.6 km2) and is located 14 miles (22km) southeast of central Austin.

Features of the Austin circuit include a distinctive 77m observation tower, the landscaped 'Grand Plaza' area, Austin360 Amphitheatre and the permanent main grandstand, which holds 9000 fans.

Over 400,000 fans flocked to the Austin circuit over the race weekend, making it one of Formula 1's best attended events in history.

No American driver has won the United States Grand Prix when it was part of the F1 World.

Circuit of The Americas is one of only five anti-clockwise tracks on the current F1 calendar (the others are Baku, Singapore, Abu Dhabi and Brazil).

Kimi Raikkonen won the 2018 US Grand Prix after a 114-race win drought; the longest such drought in F1 history.

Mercedes: The German team manufactures its own engines and has the best product on the grid.

Ferrari: Just like their rivals Mercedes, Ferrari manufactures their own engines.

Red Bull: Honda has been supplying the engine to the Austrian side since 2019.

McLaren: The Formula 1 veterans are in a deal with Renault for engines, but it will discontinue next season, and the British team will start buying engines from Mercedes in 2023.

Renault: The French team is another team on the grid, which manufactures their own engines.

Racing Point: Racing Point has been using Mercedes engines for many years and plans to continue the alliance with them in coming years.

Alfa Romeo: The Swiss team uses the Ferrari engine and has been in alliance with the F1 giants since long.

Alpha Tauri: Alpha Tauri is another team under the Red Bull brand, they unofficially work as a feeder club to the Austrian side and just like their big brothers they use Honda engines.

Haas: The only American team on the grid are the second customers of Ferrari ever since they made their debut in Formula 1 in 2016.

Williams: Apart from Racing Point, Williams also uses the Mercedes engine.

In an f1 engine revving at 18000 rpm, piston travels up and down 300 times a second.

If a connecting rod let go of its piston at max speed, the piston would have enough energy to travel vertically over 100 meters.

If a water hose were to blow off, complete cooling system would empty in just over a second.

F1 cars have 3 built in pneumatic jacks and F1 car has as many as 8 radios operating at a time.

The most powerful McLaren Formula 1 car is the 2005 MP4-20A, which had a power output of 920 bhp.

A plank of wood is bolted to the underside of every F1 car. This is to ensure the teams don't run their cars too low to the ground, which increases speed.

Lotus Racing claims its supercomputer can execute 38 trillion calculations per second.

While aeroplanes use their wings to lift them into the air, F1 cars use theirs to create downforce.

Gear changes take 30 milliseconds, 10X faster than a blink of an eye.

The fuel burning efficiency is around 99%, that's why they travel close to 300 kmph.

Formula One cars don't have air bags which normal road cars have but the cockpit walls can withstand impacts equivalent to 250 tonnes.

Since F1 cars are extremely compact, a driver removes the steering wheel to get in and out of the cockpit.

The F1 car will be able to brake from a speed of around 100 km/h to stop in 15 meters.

A Formula One tire is filled with nitrogen instead of air. As a result, the pressure is kept constant even under extreme loads.

There are 7 types of tires used in F1 races.

When a car is driving in the wet, the tyres funnel away 250 litres of water every second.

F1 drivers and mechanics wear clothes (overalls) made of Nomex which is a brand fibre that can survive for 11 seconds in temperatures of 840°C.

The tires on a F1 race car are of the highest quality rubber compounds available although highly regulated by Formula 1 tech inspection.

All teams must buy all tires which are certified and serialized direct from Pirelli.

On an average, the driver changes the gears 3000–3500 times in a single race.

A modern F1 engine consumes about 450 litres of air every second with race fuel consumption around 75 litre per 100 km.

Before the Monaco Grand prix, manhole covers are welded down because the down force created by an F1 car has enough suction to rip them off.

The pump used in F1 for refuelling can supply 12 litres of fuel per second. It would take just 4 seconds to fill an average 50 litre family car.

Pirelli supplied Formula 1 with 33,200 tyres this year. (2022).

Over the course of a 19-race season, all the cars on the grid burn approximately the same amount of fuel as a Boeing 747 Jumbo Jet does on a single flight from London to Tokyo.

If an F1 car is assembled 99.9% correctly, it would go on the track with 80 components wrongly placed.

The cars have more than a kilometre of cable linked to about 100 sensors and actuators which monitor and control the car.

F1 cars also have small wheels which switch from 13" to 18" in diameter.

The average price of an F1 engine costs $10.5 million.

The average price of an F1 exhaust costs $230,000.

The DRS overtaking aid costs $200,000.

The DRS can only be used once a driver has closed to within a second of the car ahead at a specified 'detection point' on the circuit.

The DRS was introduced in 2011.

Lewis Hamilton first took part in the F1 in 2007.

Ferrari was so dominant as a team in the early 2000s that they won the Constructors' Championship titles consecutively from 2000-2004.

In the last season of 2021, Max Verstappen clinched the title from Lewis Hamilton in the last lap of the last race in Abu Dhabi. This was the young Dutch Red Bull driver's first title.

The winner receives 25 points, the second-place finisher 18 points, with 15, 12, 10, 8, 6, 4, 2 and 1 points for positions 3 through 10, respectively.

Recording 365,000 spectators, the 2021 British Grand Prix broke attendance records.

Besides his native German, Sebastian Vettel speaks English, French, Finnish and Italian.

Max Verstappen is The youngest to ever start a Grand Prix at 17 years and 166 days.

In 2016 Formula One imposed a minimum age limit of 18 years old.

Hamilton has 103 Grand prix wins and 183 podiums.

Hamilton's Win % from 2007 - 2022 is 35.27%.

Schumacher and Vettel hold the record for most wins in a season tied at 13.

Max Verstappen become the youngest winner of a grand prix at 18 years and 228 days old for the 2016 Spanish Grand Prix.

French driver Romain Grosjean went the most races without a pole position with 181 entries.

Hamilton has a 20.21% of fastest laps over his career. 292 starts with 59 fastest laps.

After 113 races, Jenson Button won his first grand prix in 2006 season.

Perez scored 3 podiums in 2016 and outperformed his highly profiled team mate Nico Hulkenberg.

The average annual cost of running a team is approximately US$247 million.

British drivers won nine Drivers' Championships and British teams won fourteen Constructors' Championship titles between 1958 and 1974.

During 1962, Lotus introduced a car with an aluminium sheet monocoque chassis instead of the traditional space frame design. This proved to be the greatest technological breakthrough since the introduction of mid-engined cars.

Beginning in the 1970s, Bernie Ecclestone rearranged the management of Formula One's commercial rights; he is widely credited with transforming the sport into the multibillion-dollar business it now is.

On the track, the McLaren and Williams teams dominated the 1980s and 1990s.

In 2008 and 2009, Honda, BMW, and Toyota all withdrew from Formula One racing within the space of a year, blaming the economic recession.

Each driver may use no more than thirteen sets of dry-weather tyres, four sets of intermediate tyres, and three sets of wet-weather tyres during a race weekend.

Race officials may end the race early (putting out a red flag) due to unsafe conditions such as extreme rainfall.

In the 1950s, race distances varied from 300 km (190 mi) to 600 km (370 mi).

Every team in Formula One must run two cars in every session in a Grand Prix weekend, and every team may use up to four drivers in a season.

Seven out of the ten teams competing in Formula 1 are based close to London in an area centred around Oxford.

Ferrari have both their chassis and engine assembly in Maranello, Italy.

The Alpha Tauri team are based close to Ferrari in Faenza.

The Alfa Romeo team are based near Zurich in Switzerland.

Each driver chooses an unassigned number from 2 to 99 (excluding 17 which was retired following the death of Jules Bianchi).

Six of the original seven races took place in Europe.

Formula One cars must have four wheels made of the same metallic material, which must be one of two magnesium alloys specified by the FIA.

Carbon-carbon disc brakes are used for reduced weight and increased frictional performance.

A Formula 1 race car uses a hydraulically assisted Rack and Pinion steering assembly to steer the car.

An F1 steering wheel can have many different functions of buttons on the steering.

The Mercedes steering wheel was modified to have 25 buttons in 2019 and has been kept the same since.

Lewis Hamilton requested less modifications for the steering wheel so that it could be kept simple.

As of the 2022 Australian Grand Prix, there have been 771 Formula One drivers.

41 different nationalities have raced the Formula One circuit.

Since the first F1 event of the 1950 British Grand Prix there have been 1060 different races up until the start of the 2022 season.

Refuelling was banned at the end of the 2009 season as part of efforts to reduce costs and increase safety.

Formula 1 cars zig zag for multiple reasons. The main reasons for the swerving include heating the tires and brakes during the formation before race start, cleaning the tires of any debris picked up on the track, and to reduce weight by burning extra fuel.

From 1952 until 2011 Woodcote was Silverstone's final bend, but for the inaugural world championship event the sweeping right hander was the 4.6km circuit's first corner – and thus the first corner tackled in the history of F1 racing.

A Thai Prince named Prince Birabongse Bhanudej Bhanubandh (better known as Prince Bira or B. Bira) took part in the first even F1 race at Silverstone.

For the very first world championship race the average age was a mature 39 as three of the 21-driver field at Silverstone were in their fifties.

Functions Of Buttons On The Steering Wheel

Yellow N button: Selects neutral from 1st or 2nd gear.

BRKBAL (brake balance) rotary switch: Adjusts the front and rear brake balance.

Black Box button: Confirms the driver's intention to come to the pits.

Blue and orange S1/S2 buttons: These can be programmed for various functions.

Entry rotary switch: This allows the driver to make changes to corner entry settings of the differential.

Orange and green BRK-/BRK+ buttons: These change the brake balance between a programmed position and the current BRKBAL rotary position.

IGN (ignition) rotary switch: Controls ignition timing.

White ACK (acknowledge) button: Acknowledges changes in the system.

PREL (preload) rotary switch:
Controls the preload
differential offset torque.

Red Oil button: Transfers oil from
the auxiliary tank to the main tank.

Black BP (bite point) button:
Activates the clutch bite
point finding procedure.

DRS (drag reduction system) button,
upper left edge of the wheel: Activates
the rear wing flap in the DRS zone.

Red PL (pit lane) button: Activates the pit lane speed limiter, limiting the car to the designated pit lane speed limit (typically 100 km/hr).

Black R button: Activates the driver radio transmission.

SOC rotary switch: Controls the state of charge of the ERS energy storage system, whether the system is generating or consuming energy.

Pedal rotary switch: Changes the pedal map dictating how the accelerator pedal responds to inputs.

Fuel rotary switch: Controls the rate of fuel consumption.

Black OT button: Activates configurable performance maps to assist the driver in overtaking or defending.

Tire rotary switch: Tells the ECU and other systems what type of tire the car is running on.

BBal-/BBal+ switches: These are used to make fine adjustments to the brake balance offset.

Scan The QR Code To Check Out More Utopia Press Books On Amazon!

Printed in Great Britain
by Amazon